the cocktail
hour

the cocktail hour

ben reed

photography by william lingwood

RYLAND
PETERS
& SMALL

LONDON NEW YORK

Senior Designer Susan Downing
Editor Miriam Hyslop
Production Tamsin Curwood
Art Director Gabriella Le Grazie
Publishing Director Alison Starling

Mixologist Ben Reed
Stylist Helen Trent

First published in Great Britain in 2002
by Ryland Peters & Small
Kirkman House
12–14 Whitfield Street
London W1T 2RP
www.rylandpeters.com

10 9 8 7 6 5 4 3 2

ISBN 1 84172 321 5
A CIP record for this book is available from the British Library.
Printed in China.

contents

the cocktail hour

The origin of the cocktail is steeped in colourful myth. It has a number of explanations for its derivation. Among my favourites is the story of the publican who, during the American War of Independence lost one of his finest fighting cockerels. He was inconsolable until the day an army lieutenant came riding into town with the bird. The publican immediately mixed up a special concoction (no doubt containing Kentucky whiskey) and served it to the soldier, toasting him with the phrase 'to the cock's tail' (for returning the bird with all the feathers in its tail intact).

Although many of the cocktails we regard today as 'classic' were invented before the 20th century, it was during the roaring twenties that cocktails came into their own. Immortalized on the silver screen, with dialogue smattered with references to champagne cocktails and martinis, they became the drink of the chic and sophisticated. Ironically it was prohibition and the abundance of bootleg or bathtub liqueur that forced the alcohol-friendly masses to invent mixes, which first took the sting out of the illicit spirits and secondly confused the authorities raiding the speakeasies.

Today, the true classic is a drink of subtlety and depth of taste, where one ingredient perfectly complements another to create an elixir of no more than two alcoholic ingredients.

The methods of preparation are often hugely contentious – think martini with the ubiquitous 'shaken' or 'stirred' argument. Invariably, and this is the joy with timeless cocktails, when a cocktail can be made in a number of ways, a new title is often bestowed upon the drink and a new life given!

As cocktails and cocktail drinkers evolve, we, as the drinks enthusiasts of the world, should always cherish the classic, as it gives us the foundation to both toast the past and mix for the future.

EQUIPMENT

The first thing any aspiring bartender should acquire is a **measure (jigger)**. Too many professional bartenders regard the jigger as a tool for the novice – their guesswork results in many delicate cocktails being ruined. The modern dual-measure jigger measures both 50 ml and 25 ml (a double and a single measure). The **shaker** is the second most important piece of equipment for a bartender. The **barspoon**, with its long spiralling handle, is useful for stirring drinks and for the gentle pouring required for layered drinks. The 'wrong', flat end can

equipment
and
techniques

be used for muddling or crushing herbs, etc. A **muddler**, a wooden pestle for mixing or crushing sugar cubes, limes and herbs, etc, and the **bartender's friend** for opening cans and removing corks and bottle caps, are also handy. A **mixing glass** with strainer is used for making drinks that are stirred, not shaken. Other useful but not essential accessories include an **ice bucket**, **ice tongs** and a **juice squeezer**.

GLASSES

The traditional **martini glass** is a very familiar icon, with its open face and slim stem. The **cocktail glass** is similar to the martini glass but with a slightly rounded bowl.

The **rocks** or **old fashioned glass** is a squat, straight-sided glass, which sits on a heavy base and feels comfortable in the hand. The **highball** and the **collins glasses** come in various sizes but they are all tall, slim glasses designed to keep a long drink fresh and cold. The small, sturdy **shot glass** is designed with one purpose: getting the drink from one's glass into one's mouth with minimal fuss.

The **champagne flute** is perfect for keeping the sparkle in your champagne cocktails. It should be elegant and long-stemmed, with a narrow rim to enhance the delicacy of the drink.

TECHNIQUES

There are six basic ways of creating a cocktail: **building**, **blending**, **shaking**, **stirring over ice**, **layering** and **muddling**. Whichever method you are using, accurately measure the ingredients first to get that all-important balance of tastes right. If you would rather try guesswork just see how much practice it takes to get the quantity right to fill the glass exactly – I still have problems in that department! The process of **building** a cocktail just requires adding the measured ingredients to the appropriate glass, with ice, and giving it a quick stir before serving. The **blending** method involves pouring all the ingredients into a blender, adding crushed ice and flicking the switch. Using a **shaker** is the most enjoyable way to mix a cocktail, both for you and your guests. Add the ingredients to the shaker and fill it with ice. The shaking movement should be sharp and fairly assertive, but do remember to keep your hands on both parts of the shaker or at least a finger on the cap. Drinks containing egg white, cream and juices should be shaken for slightly longer than the usual ten seconds. **Stirring** is the best method when you want to retain the clarity and strength of the spirits. Manhattans, for example, are always stirred. Use an ice-filled mixing glass and stir carefully to avoid chipping the ice and diluting the drink. Frost your serving glasses by leaving them in the freezer for an hour before use. **Layering** is the technique used for drinks such as the White Russian. With the flat end of a barspoon resting on the surface of the base spirit, pour each of the remaining spirits in turn down the handle of the spoon. This keeps the ingredients separate and allows them to be tasted one at a time. The **muddling** technique involves using the flat end of a barspoon or a muddler to mix or crush ingredients such as fruit or herbs and allow the flavours to be released gently.

Pink Gin is a thoroughly British cocktail which deserves a premium gin. Although it originated as a medicinal potion in the British Navy, Pink Gin became one of the smartest drinks in 1940s' London.

pink
gin

50 ml gin
a dash of Angostura bitters

Rinse a frosted sherry or martini glass with Angostura bitters, add chilled gin and serve.

GIN

classic
dry
martini

50 ml gin
a dash of dry vermouth
green olive

Using a mixing glass, chill
the gin and vermouth over
ice and pour into a frosted
martini glass. Garnish with
a green olive.

The **Classic Dry Martini** has long been considered the ultimate in sophistication and elegance. Its roots date back as far as the 1840s where it is believed to have been served at a bar in Martinez, California. The **FDR** (so named after President Roosevelt) and the **Smoky Martini** are popular variations on the stylish classic.

fdr
martini

ALSO KNOWN AS THE DIRTY MARTINI
50 ml gin
a dash of dry vermouth
12.5 ml olive brine
green olive

Add the gin, a dash of dry vermouth and the olive brine to a shaker filled with cracked ice. Shake sharply and strain into a frosted martini glass. Garnish with an olive. Made to Mr. Roosevelt's specifications!

smoky
martini

50 ml gin
a dash of dry vermouth
a dash of whisky

This is a variation on the FDR Martini, with the whisky substituting for the olive brine, but the method is identical.

silver bronx

50 ml gin
a dash of dry vermouth
a dash of sweet vermouth
50 ml fresh orange juice
1 egg white

Shake all the ingredients
vigorously over ice and strain
into a chilled cocktail glass.

golden bronx

The method is the same as
above, but substitute the egg
white for an egg yolk.

The **Bronx** dates back to the
days of Prohibition, when gang
bosses reigned and booze played
an important part in the economy
of the underworld. Different areas
of New York became known
for the special cocktails they
offered, such as this speciality
of the Bronx district. Like the
Manhattan, it has three variations:
the dry, the sweet and the
perfect. The **Silver** and **Golden
Bronx** are variations on the
perfect, with the addition of
egg white or egg yolk.

gin gimlet

50 ml gin
25 ml lime cordial

Pour the gin and cordial into a shaker filled with ice. Shake very sharply and strain through a sieve into a frosted martini glass.

Made popular during in the 1930s, the **Gin Gimlet** should be shaken vigorously to ensure that the cocktail is chilled to perfection, then strained carefully before serving to catch any chips of ice. The **Journalist**, another classic gin cocktail, is a good pre-dinner drink to order at a bar. If you are making a Journalist at home watch the measurements carefully; it's a drink that needs to be very finely balanced.

the
journalist

25 ml gin

a dash of sweet vermouth

a dash of dry vermouth

2 dashes of fresh lemon juice

2 dashes of triple sec

2 dashes of Angostura bitters

Shake all the ingredients over ice
and strain into a frosted martini glass.

Two offshoots of the original Gin Fizz, (a classic that some would say should remain untouched) these cocktails have now become classics in their own right. The substitution of the soda by champagne in the **Royal Gin Fizz** helps to make it special and lends it a little extra fizz (surely no harm there!). The addition of the rose flower water in the **New Orleans** or **Ramos Fizz** accentuates the juniper flavour in the gin and the dash of cream gives this very light drink a little more body.

royal gin fizz

50 ml gin
25 ml fresh lemon juice
1 barspoon white sugar
   (or 12.5 ml sugar syrup)
champagne
1 egg white

Put the egg white, gin, lemon juice and sugar into a shaker filled with ice and shake vigorously. Strain into a collins glass filled with ice. Top with champagne.

new orleans fizz

ALSO KNOWN AS THE RAMOS FIZZ

50 ml gin
25 ml fresh lemon juice
1 barspoon white sugar
   (or 12.5 ml sugar syrup)
12.5 ml rose flower water
   (or orange flower water)
12.5 ml single cream
a dash of egg white
soda water

Add all the ingredients, except the soda water, to a shaker filled with ice. Shake vigorously and strain into a highball over ice. Gently add the soda water, stirring with a barspoon while doing so.

VODKA

The **Black** and **White Russians** are classics that have been on the scene since the Cold War era. They make stylish after-dinner cocktails with their sweet coffee flavour, which is sharpened up by the vodka. The White Russian, with its addition of the cream float, is even more appropriate as a nightcap.

black russian

50 ml vodka
25 ml Kahlúa coffee liqueur
stemmed cherry

Shake the vodka and Kahlúa together over ice and strain into a rocks glass filled with ice. Garnish with a stemmed cherry.

white
russian

For a White Russian, layer 25 ml single cream into the glass of Black Russian over the back of a barspoon. Garnish with a stemmed cherry.

silver
streak

25 ml chilled vodka
25 ml kümmel

Pour a generous single measure
of chilled vodka into a rocks glass
filled with ice. Add a similar amount
of kümmel, stir gently and serve.

A classic in its own right, the first **Vodkatini** dates back to the 1950s. As with the Classic Dry Martini, there are four important things to consider when it comes to making it: the quantity of vermouth, to shake or stir, straight up or on the rocks, and lastly, an olive or a twist. The **Silver Streak** features the liqueur kümmel, and has a distinctive, aniseed-like taste that comes from the caraway seeds used in its production.

vodkatini

50 ml vodka
a dash of dry vermouth
pitted olive or lemon zest

Fill a mixing glass with ice and stir with a barspoon until the glass is chilled. Tip the water out and top with ice. Add a dash of dry vermouth and continue stirring. Strain the liquid away and top with ice. Add a large measure of vodka and stir in a continuous circular motion until the vodka is thoroughly chilled (taking care not to chip the ice and dilute the vodka). Strain into a frosted martini glass and garnish with either a pitted olive or a twist of lemon zest.

50 ml vodka
12.5 ml Galliano
fresh orange juice
orange slice

Pour a large measure of vodka into a highball glass filled with ice. Fill the glass almost to the top with orange juice and pour in a float of Galliano. Garnish with an orange slice and serve with a swizzle stick and straw.

harvey wallbanger

The story goes that Harvey, a Californian surfer
who had performed particularly badly in an
important contest, visited his local bar to drown
his sorrows. He ordered his usual screwdriver –
only to decide that it wasn't strong enough
for what he had in mind. Scanning the bar for
something to boost his drink, his eyes fell on the
distinctively shaped Galliano bottle, a shot of
which was then added to his drink as a float.
Needless to say, his resultant state after a few
of these was so rocky that, as he searched
for the door on the way out, he bounced off a
couple of walls before spilling out onto the street.
Harvey Wallbanger they called him.

moscow
mule

50 ml vodka
1 lime
ginger beer

Pour a large measure of vodka
into a highball filled with ice.
Cut the lime into quarters,
squeeze and drop into the glass.
Top with ginger beer and stir with
a barspoon. Serve with a straw.

The creation of the **Moscow Mule** celebrates the godsend
that is ginger beer. It lends the Mule its legendary kick and an
easy spiciness. The **Bloody Mary** has been a renowned hang-
over cure or pick-me-up for years. Curing hangovers can be
painless, and should be enjoyable too. They are an aspect of
bartending that cannot be ignored – and, in a truly biblical
way, what the bartender giveth so shall he take away.

bloody
mary

50 ml vodka
200 ml tomato juice
2 grinds of black pepper
2 dashes of Worcestershire sauce
2 dashes of Tabasco sauce
2 dashes of fresh lemon juice
1 barspoon horseradish sauce
1 celery stick

Shake all the ingredients over ice and strain
into a highball glass filled with ice. Garnish
with a celery stick. (These measurements are
dependent on personal likes for spices.)

WHISKY

The naming of Manhattan Island has an anecdotal history that links it with the cocktail. 'Manhachtanienck' roughly translates as 'the island where we became intoxicated', so named in the early 17th century by Lenape Indians after drinking a dark spirit.

50 ml rye whiskey
25 ml dry vermouth
a dash of Angostura bitters
lemon zest

dry manhattan

For each of the variations, add the ingredients to a mixing glass filled with ice (ensure all ingredients are very cold) and stir the mixture until chilled. Strain into a frosted martini glass, add the garnish and serve.

perfect
manhattan

50 ml rye whiskey
12.5 ml sweet vermouth
12.5 ml dry vermouth
a dash of Angostura bitters
maraschino cherry

sweet
manhattan

50 ml rye whiskey
25 ml sweet vermouth
a dash of orange bitters
orange zest

old fashioned

50 ml bourbon
1 white sugar cube
2 dashes of orange bitters
orange zest

Place the sugar cube soaked with orange bitters into a rocks glass, muddle the mixture with a barspoon and add a dash of bourbon and a couple of ice cubes. Keep adding ice and bourbon and keep muddling until the full 50 ml has been added to the glass (ensuring the sugar has dissolved). Rim the glass with a strip of orange and drop it into the glass.

The **Old Fashioned**, the **Mint Julep** and the **Rusty Nail** have one thing in common – they are all timeless whisky cocktails that never fail to delight. As those among us who are already connoisseurs of the water of life will tell you, each cocktail should be serenaded with a few gentle words of seduction, sipped, and finally, savoured.

mint julep

50 ml bourbon
2 sugar cubes
5 sprigs of mint

Crush the mint and sugar cubes in the bottom of a collins glass. Fill the glass with crushed ice and add the bourbon. Stir the mixture vigorously with a barspoon and serve.

rusty nail

30 ml whisky
30 ml Drambuie
orange zest

Add both ingredients to a glass filled with ice and muddle with a barspoon. Garnish with a zest of orange.

boston
sour

50 ml bourbon
25 ml fresh lemon juice
2 barspoons sugar syrup
2 dashes of Angostura bitters
a dash of egg white
lemon slice and maraschino cherry

Add all the ingredients to a shaker filled
with ice and shake sharply. Strain the
contents into a whisky tumbler filled
with ice, garnish with a lemon slice and
a maraschino cherry.

new orleans
sazerac

Reputed to be the very first cocktail, the **Sazerac** has been around since the 1830s. To fully enjoy its flavours the Sazerac should be drunk undiluted. The classic Sour is made with Scotch, but since I like my sours a little on the sweet side I prefer the vanillary sweetness of this bourbon based **Boston Sour**.

50 ml bourbon
25 ml Pernod
1 sugar cube
a dash of Angostura
   bitters

Rinse an old fashioned glass with Pernod and discard the Pernod. Put the sugar in the glass, saturate with Angostura bitters, then add ice cubes and the bourbon and serve.

The **Hot Toddy**, with its warming blend of spices and sweet honey aroma, has long been the perfect comforter and will soothe any aches, snuffles and alcohol withdrawal symptoms that your illness may have inflicted upon you. It's also a great life-saver for cold afternoons spent outside watching sport. Next time you have need to pack a thermos flask of coffee, think again – mix up a batch of Hot Toddies, and see how much more popular you are than the next man!

hot toddy

50 ml whisky
25 ml fresh lemon juice
2 barspoons honey or sugar syrup
75 ml hot water
1 cinnamon stick
5 whole cloves
2 lemon slices

Spear the cloves into the lemon slices and add them to a heatproof glass or a toddy glass along with the rest of the ingredients.

The **Mai Tai** was originally made in the 1940s by Victor Bergeron (Trader Vic) in California. With its complex mixture of flavours it has as many variations as it has garnishes. The one thing that most bartenders seem to agree on is that a thick, dark rum should be used, along with all the fruit-based ingredients that lend the classic its legendary fruitiness.

mai tai

25 ml Demerara rum
25 ml gold rum
25 ml orange curaçao
12.5 ml apricot brandy
12.5 ml fresh lemon or lime juice
a dash of Angostura bitters
2 dashes of orgeat syrup
50 ml fresh pineapple juice
a mint sprig

Add all the ingredients to a cocktail shaker filled with ice, shake and strain into an ice-filled old fashioned glass. Garnish with a pineapple slice and a mint sprig. Serve with straws.

orange
daiquiri

50 ml Creole Schrubb rum
25 ml fresh lemon juice
2 barspoons sugar syrup

Measure all the ingredients and pour into an
ice-filled shaker. Shake and strain through a
sieve into a frosted martini glass.

50 ml golden rum
25 ml fresh lime juice
3 barspoons sugar syrup

Measure all the ingredients and pour
into an ice-filled shaker. Shake and
strain into a frosted martini glass.

original
daiquiri

bacardi
cocktail

50 ml Bacardi white rum

a dash of grenadine

juice of 1 small lime

1 barspoon of powdered sugar or
  a dash of sugar syrup

Shake all the ingredients sharply
over ice, then strain into a frosted
martini glass and serve.

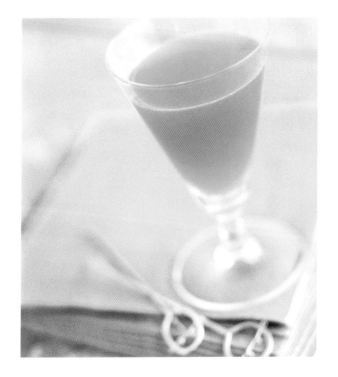

The **Original Daiquiri** is a classic cocktail that was made famous in the El Floridita restaurant Havana, early in the 20th century. It has as many recipe variations as famous drinkers (Hemingway always ordered doubles at El Floridita) but once you have found the perfect balance then stick to those measurements exactly. The **Orange Daiquiri** and **Bacardi Cocktail** are two of the best-known variations.

A sweet, creamy drink that, for a time, epitomized the kind of cocktail disapproved of by 'real' cocktail drinkers (compare a **Piña Colada** with a Classic Dry Martini!). However, since its creation in the 1970s, it has won widespread popularity, and now that we are in the new millennium cocktails are for everyone, so there's no shame in ordering this modern day classic at the bar.

piña colada

50 ml golden rum
25 ml coconut cream
12.5 ml cream
25 ml fresh pineapple juice
a slice of pineapple

Put all the ingredients into a blender, add an ice scoop of crushed ice and blend. Pour into a sour or collins glass and garnish with a slice of pineapple.

rum
runner

25 ml white rum

25 ml dark rum

juice of 1 lime

a dash of sugar syrup

150 ml fresh pineapple juice

Shake all the ingredients sharply over ice in a shaker and strain into a highball glass filled with crushed ice.

The **Rum Runner** is a perfect example of rum's affinity with fresh juices. Rum also has the ability to hold its own when combined with quite a selection of other flavours. The **Planter's Punch** recipe can never be forgotten since Myers has very kindly put the recipe on the back label of its rum bottle. A great favourite for parties because it can be made in advance, Planter's Punch can be prepared in an old oak barrel for authenticity but a big bowl will do, with slices of fruit added, such as oranges, melons, apples and pears. The **T-Punch** is a refreshing drink, perfect for a hot summer day, and can be made according to taste with more lime or more sugar for a quick variation.

planter's punch

50 ml Myers rum
juice of half a lemon
50 ml fresh orange juice
a dash of sugar syrup
soda water
orange slice

Pour all the ingredients, except the soda water, into a cocktail shaker filled with ice, shake and strain into a ice-filled highball. Top up with soda water and garnish with a slice of orange.

t-punch

50 ml white rum
1 lime
1 brown sugar cube
soda water

Place the sugar cube in the bottom of an old fashioned glass. Cut the lime into eighths, squeeze and drop into the glass. Pound with a pestle to break up the sugar. Add the rum and ice, then top up with soda water. Stir and serve.

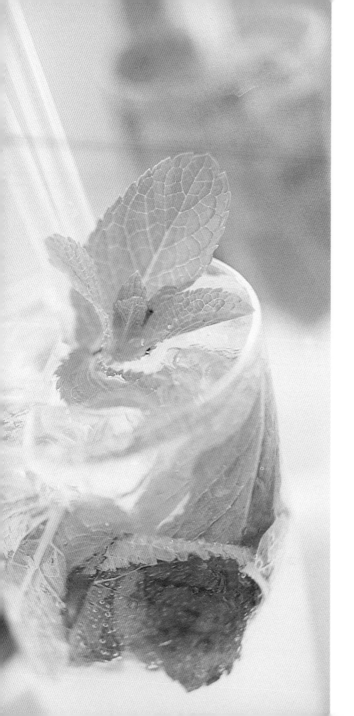

The **Mojito**, with its alluring mix of mint and rum, invariably whisks its drinker away to warmer climes. Championed by Hemmingway in the 1940s and wildly popular in Miami for years, this Cuban concoction can now be found gracing the menus of discerning cocktail bars around the world.

mojito

50 ml golden rum
5 sprigs of mint
2 dashes of sugar syrup
a dash of fresh lime juice
soda water

Put the mint into a highball, add the rum, lime juice and sugar syrup and pound with a barspoon until the aroma of the mint is released. Add the crushed ice and stir vigorously until the mixture and the mint is spread evenly. Top with soda water and stir again. Serve with straws.

cuba
libre

50 ml white rum
1 lime
cola

Pour the rum into a highball
filled with ice; cut a lime into
eighths, squeeze and drop the
wedges into the glass. Top with
cola and serve with straws.

One of the most famous of all rum-based drinks the **Cuba Libra** was reputed to have been invented by an army officer in Cuba shortly after Coca Cola was first produced in the 1890s. Cachaça, a spirit indigenous to Brazil is distilled directly from the juice of sugar cane, unlike white rum, which is usually distilled from molasses. The **Caipirinha** has made cachaça popular in many countries.

caipirinha

50 ml cachaça
1 lime
2 brown sugar cubes

Cut the lime into eighths, squeeze and place into an old fashioned glass with the sugar cubes, then pound well with a pestle. Fill the glass with crushed ice and add the cachaça. Stir vigorously and serve with a straw.

50 ml gold tequila
50 ml champagne (chilled)

Pour both the tequila and
the chilled champagne
into a small collins glass
with a sturdy base. Hold a
napkin over the glass
(sealing the liquid inside),
sharply slam the glass
down onto a stable
surface and drink in one
go while it is still fizzing.

tequila slammer

margarita

50 ml gold tequila
25 ml triple sec (or Cointreau)
juice of half a lime

Shake all the ingredients
sharply with cracked ice.
Strain into a chilled cocktail
glass rimmed with salt.

The **Margarita** is the cocktail most closely associated with tequila. This is the classic recipe, but when you are making it at home there is no right or wrong way – just your way! You can use Cointreau or triple sec, lime or lemon juice or even cordial, but never, ever use a ready-made premix.

The **Tequila Slammer** is a drink that needs to be handled with care. This one is more likely to be imbibed for the sensation rather than the taste!

BRANDY, LIQUEURS & APERITIFS

brandy alexander

50 ml brandy
12.5 ml crème de cacao
  (dark and white)
12.5 ml double cream
nutmeg

Shake all the ingredients over
ice and strain into a frosted
martini glass. Garnish with
a sprinkle of nutmeg.

The **Brandy Alexander** is the perfect

after-dinner cocktail, luscious and

seductive and great for chocolate lovers.

It's important, though, to get the

proportions right so that the brandy

stands out as the major investor.

stinger

50 ml brandy
25 ml crème de menthe (white)

Shake the ingredients together
over ice and strain into a frosted
martini glass.

The **Stinger** is a great palate cleanser
and digestif and, like brandy, should be
consumed after dinner. The amount of crème
de menthe added depends on personal taste.
The **Sidecar**, like many of the classic cocktails
created in the 1920s, is attributed to the
inventive genius of Harry MacElhone, who
founded Harry's New York Bar in Paris. It is
said to have been created in honour of an
eccentric military man who would roll up outside
the bar in the sidecar of his chauffeur-driven
motorcycle. It is certainly the cocktail choice
of people who know precisely what they want.

50 ml brandy
juice of half a lemon
12.5 ml Cointreau

Shake all the ingredients
together over ice and strain
into a frosted martini glass
with a sugared rim.

sidecar

25 ml Campari
25 ml sweet vermouth
soda water
1 orange slice

Build the ingredients over ice
into a highball glass, stir and
serve with an orange slice.

americano

The **Americano** and the **Negroni** have, of course, been around for a long time. The Americano is a refreshing blend of bitter and sweet, topped with soda to make the perfect thirst quencher for a hot summer afternoon. The Negroni packs a powerful punch but still makes an elegant aperitif. For a drier variation, add a little more dry gin, but if a fruitier cocktail is more to your taste, wipe some orange zest around the top of the glass and add some to the drink.

negroni

25 ml Campari
25 ml sweet vermouth
25 ml gin
orange zest

Build all the ingredients into a rocks glass filled with ice, garnish with a twist of orange zest and stir well. For an extra-dry Negroni, add a little more gin.

The **Golden Cadillac** is not a drink to be approached lightly, and you could be excused for raising your eyebrows at the possibility of mixing crème de cacao (chocolate flavoured) with orange juice and Galliano (herb and liquorice flavoured). If the thought of this combination is too much for you, try substituting the crème de cacao with Cointreau to create another popular cocktail called Golden Dream. The **Grasshopper** is a more obvious combination of peppermint and cream, the perfect drink for after dinner.

golden
cadillac

25 ml crème de cacao (white)
25 ml single cream
50 ml fresh orange juice
a dash of Galliano

Shake all the ingredients over ice, strain into a martini glass and serve.

grasshopper

25 ml crème de menthe (white)
12.5 ml crème de menthe (green)
25 ml single cream

Shake all the ingredients over ice, strain into a frosted martini glass and serve.

CHAMPAGNE

25 ml brandy
1 white sugar cube
2 dashes of Angostura bitters
dry champagne

Moisten the sugar cube with
Angostura bitters and place in
a champagne flute. Add the
brandy, then gently pour in
the champagne and serve.

champagne
cocktail

This cocktail has truly stood the test of time,

as popular now as when it was sipped by

the stars of the silver screen in the 1940s.

It's a simple and delicious cocktail that

epitomizes the elegance and sophistication

of that era and still lends that same touch of

urbanity to those who drink it today.

If there is another drink in the world that looks more tempting and drinkable than a **Black Velvet**, then please, someone make it for me now. Pour this drink gently into the glass to allow for the somewhat unpredictable nature of both the Guinness and the champagne. The **Bellini** originated in Harry's Bar in Venice in the early 1940s and became a favourite of the movers and shakers of chic society. Although there are many variations on this recipe, there is one golden rule for the perfect Bellini – always use fresh, ripe peaches to make the peach juice.

black
velvet

Guinness
champagne

Half fill a champagne flute with Guinness, gently top with champagne and serve.

bellini

¼ fresh peach, skinned
12.5 ml crème de pèche
a dash of peach
   bitters (optional)
champagne
peach ball

Blend the peach and add
to a champagne flute.
Pour in the crème de pèche
and the peach bitters,
if using, and gently top up
with champagne, stirring
carefully and continuously.
Garnish with a peach ball
in the bottom of the glass,
then serve.

25 ml vodka
1 white sugar cube
2 dashes of Angostura bitters
champagne

Moisten the sugar cube with
Angostura bitters and put into a
martini glass. Cover the sugar
cube with the vodka and top
with champagne.

james bond

french 75

50 ml gin
25 ml fresh lemon juice
12.5 ml sugar syrup
champagne
lemon zest

Shake the gin, lemon juice and
sugar syrup over ice and strain
into a champagne flute. Top with
champagne and garnish with a
long strip of lemon zest.

The **James Bond** is a variation on the
Champagne Cocktail, using vodka instead
of the more traditional brandy. The naming
of this cocktail is a mystery to me since the
eponymous spy liked his drinks shaken!

The **French 75** is another classic cocktail from
Harry's New York Bar in Paris. It's not dissimilar
to a Gin Sling, but is topped up with champagne
instead of soda water.

index